ACKNOWLEDGEMENTS

Editor and Publisher: Andrew D. Gordon

Tablature Assistant: Vic Martinez

Rhythmic Notation Assistant: Mark Fitchett

Computer Score Copyist: Jeremy Ives of n th. Generation Graphics using Finale scoring software

Graphic Artist: Janice Watson **Watson Design**

Photography: **Skupenski**

Proof Reader: Suzanne Sawyer

Recording Studio: Leigh Genniss, Soundwriter Recording Studios, Manhattan Beach, CA.

Barry Levenson plays **Fender** guitars and amplifiers and uses **SIT** strings.

This book is dedicated to my father Fred Levenson for always encouraging people to pursue the things in life that they love, and also to all the great artists of American music.

Printed in the U.S.A.

1

INTRODUCTION

My almost twenty- year relationship with the Blues has involved countless numbers of gigs, working and recording with many of the giants in the Blues field, hours of transcribing records, and teaching many wonderful and inspirational students.

These experiences have given me definite ideas about a teaching method that reveals the essence of constructing concise, coherent and melodically structured solos (improvisations), enabling the aspiring musician to develop a strong foundation for self exploration and expression.

I realized, after analyzing the solos of the masters, that regardless of the genre of music, all great improvisers had three common qualities inherent in their playing:

1. The use of motific development (A "motif" being a melodic or rhythmic phrase that is repeated, perhaps with slight variation throughout a solo and is used to structure melodic and/ or rhythmic continuity, development and theme).

2. Playing a solo over the chord changes. Melodic ideas that are built from using the notes in the chord that is being improvised on.

3. The mastery of scales, arpeggios and passing tones.

Besides having the required techniques needed for self expression, the truly great players have mastered the three aforementioned concepts.

When I first started to teach Blues improvisation, it soon became apparent to me that while I could teach licks, guitar techniques and note for note transcribed solos, this was not giving my students the understanding of spontaneous composition i.e. creating their own solos. They either played the Blues and Pentatonic scales,or their favorite licks over and over without regard to phrasing, rhythm or chord changes. (Thus became the seed of this book.) I composed a series of solos that were built strictly upon the principles of motific development and utilized the notes and chords of the Blues progression. These fourteen solo examples were written specifically with the intent of exploring the strongest principles of Blues improvisation. This includes melody, phrasing, motific development, chordal reinforcement and techniques inherent to the guitar. I also made sure that these solos were composed of many of the greatest licks that are associated with Blues guitar playing. Careful study and analysis of the concepts in these solos lead the aspiring student to new levels of creative improvising and a greater knowledge and understanding of the art of Blues guitar.

By analyzing the principles of solo construction the student can actually see the thinking process that goes into the making of a good solo. The idea that after this thinking process becomes second nature, the art of true improvisation becomes a reality. Using this method, the progress of my more devoted students was amazing. They were able to start playing mature sounding musical statements and could immediately incorporate any new licks into their playing and have them become a useful part of their vocabulary.

When I was approached about writing a book by my longtime friend Andrew Gordon (owner of A.D.G. PRODUCTIONS) I had been using the above teaching method for a few years with extremely successful results. I am truly pleased that this exciting method will be made available to music students around the world. I hope that it becomes a useful tool for self expression. This is a small way of paying back the many wonderful experiences I have had from my relationship with this timeless American art form called the Blues.

HOW TO USE THIS BOOK

1. Listen to the solo at least five times to familiarize yourself with the music.

2. Learn the music slowly, a few bars at a time while listening to the tape for any articulations such as bends, vibrato, slurs, hammer ons, pull offs, etc.

3. Work out any technical difficulties such as fingerings, picking, speed etc. you might encounter, before moving on to a new measure.

4. After each section is mastered, play the complete piece at a comfortable tempo.

5. Play the solo, note for note, along with the tape, paying careful attention to phrasing.

6. Play along with the rhythm track minus the solo guitar that is provided after each example.

7. When you feel you can duplicate the solo comfortably, then study the solo analysis that accompanies the solo.

8. Using the concepts and principles explored in the solo, improvise your own solo. Always strive to create musical statements.

A WORD ABOUT WRITTEN NOTATION

Because of the complex and varied rhythms involved in Blues phrasing, the fact that many Blues phrases fall "between the cracks" as opposed to being on the beat and the different ways rhythms can be notated, some of the examples in this book may at first seem difficult to read. Careful listening to the recording that accompanies the text should solve any problems that may arise in understanding the written music.

EXPLANATIONS OF TERMS AND TECHNIQUES
USED IN THE BOOK

1. The three main scales used for Blues improvising are: Blues, Minor pentatonic and Major pentatonic scale.

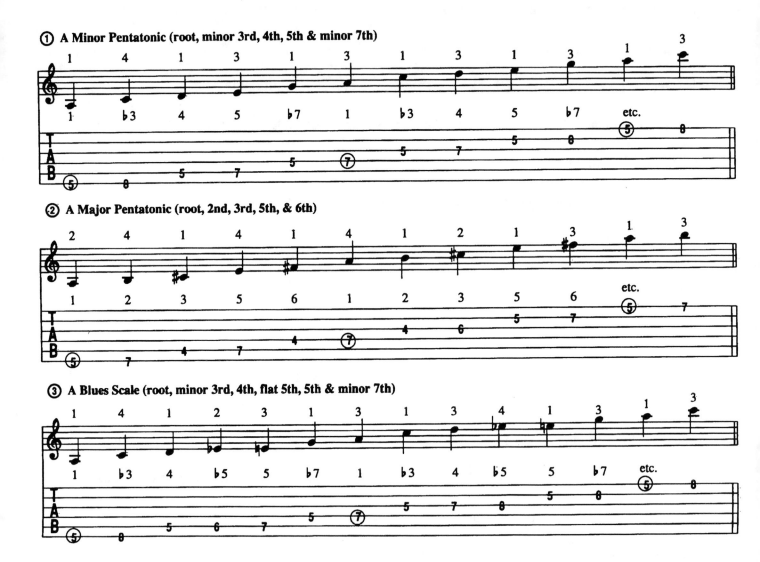

① A Minor Pentatonic (root, minor 3rd, 4th, 5th & minor 7th)

② A Major Pentatonic (root, 2nd, 3rd, 5th, & 6th)

③ A Blues Scale (root, minor 3rd, 4th, flat 5th, 5th & minor 7th)

2. HYBRID SCALES

As I stated earlier, the three most widely used scales for Blues improvisation are 1) the pentatonic major 2) pentatonic minor 3) blues scale. When we use combinations of notes from these three different scales we get "hybrid" scales and licks.

3. CHROMATIC ROW

A line that is created when certain "hybrid" scale combining occurs. The chromatic row consists of the b3 (from the minor pentatonic), major 3rd. (from the major pentatonic), the 4th. (from the minor pentatonic), the b5 (from the blues scale) and the 5th. (from all three scales). This five note chromatic line is an excellent source of improvising material and will be studied in depth in this text.

4. MOTIFS

A motif is a melodic and or rhythmic phrase that is repeated, perhaps with a slight variation throughout a solo and is used to structure melodic and or rhythmic continuity, development and theme.

5.TARGET NOTES

A large part of this text is devoted to the study of "target notes". "Target notes", quite simply are the main notes that spell out or reinforce chordal harmony. Used properly, these "target notes" outline chord changes and add melody and structure to improvisations. These notes are called "target notes" because as a rule, melodic phrases should be targeted so as to begin and or end on these notes. Mastering the use of these "target notes" is an essential part of strong Blues improvisation. Since much of this text is devoted to the study and usage of target notes this book will go a long way towards developing a complete working knowledge and understanding of this important concept.

Using an "A" Blues progression as an example, the target notes in order of importance are as follows:
I chord A7. C# (the major 3rd). G (the dominant seventh). E (the fifth). A (the root).
IVchord D7. F# (the major third). C (the dominant seventh). A (the fifth). D (the root).
V chord E7. G# (the major third). D (the dominant seventh). B (the fifth). E (the root).

6. ARPEGGIOS

Arpeggios are the notes that make up a chord played one at a time. They can be played in any order and since they outline chordal structure they are great sources of improvising material.

7. STRING BENDING

One of the most impressive characteristics idiomatic to the electric guitar is the ability to bend strings. This technique allows the player's personal touch, feelings and personality to come out in the music. The unique "pallet of sound" that can be achieved using string bending techniques can go a long way towards helping the aspiring player to develop a personal recognizable style. Blues, being such an emotional form, especially lends itself to the art of string bending. A major component that makes up the styles of the great Blues guitar players lies in their string bending ability. From the wild "overbends" of Buddy Guy and Albert King, the "singing strings" of Otis Rush, the masterful bending of B.B. King to the eccentric bends of Hubert Sumlin, Blues guitar and string bending will always be inseparable. The following photographs demonstrate some of the more effective ways to achieve proper string bending. Always strive to bend in tune. If you are bending a whole step, check yourself by playing the note you are bending to, then bend to it while listening for the proper pitch. After a while, your ear will reach a point where you will be able to hear and feel exactly how far to bend. When used properly, this technique allows one to express the full gamut of human emotions through a guitar in a most unique and wonderful way. (See photo section.)

8. VIBRATO

Hand in hand with the technique of string bending comes the art of vibrato. Vibrato lets each note have its own unique and personal identity. Vibratos are as varied and individualistic as speaking voices, which in fact is essentially what they are, when applied to the guitar. Vibrato is achieved by "pushing" or "shaking" the string in an even pulse by moving the fingers and or the wrist. This can be done either on notes that are not bent or on notes that are bent two whole steps or more. The latter obviously requires a lot more strength. When vibrato is applied to a stationary note, care must be taken to keep the note in tune. Regardless of the speed of the vibrato, the pulse should be smooth and even. Jerky uneven vibratos sound nervous and unmusical. Since vibrato is such a major factor in the development of one's personal style, care and practice should be taken to master this technique. Listening to the great players and emulating their vibratos will go a long way towards helping you to develop your own. (See photo section.)

9. SLIDES

Slides are achieved by simply running a finger up or down the strings to sound a particular note. In some cases they can be used to end a phrase with no particular sounded note, but as an exclamation point. One of the techniques explored in this text is to play a given note, bend it and slide up the string to a another given note that is either bent or not bent. This technique has a unique sound and will explored in detail in this text.

10. UNISON SLIDE

The "unison slide" is performed by playing a note on one string and sliding to the same note on an adjacent string for example: play an "A" fifth fret E string and slide to an "A" tenth fret B string. This technique is useful not only for its unique sound, but it is also an effective method for transversing position changes.

11. HAMMER-ON

A hammer-on is performed by striking the first (lower) note, then sounding the higher note with another finger by fretting it without picking.

12. PULL-OFF

A pull-off is performed by placing both fingers on the notes to be sounded, picking the first note and without picking, pulling the finger off to sound the second (lower) note.

13. TRILL

A trill is a hammer-on that is repeated over and over.

14. RAKES

A rake is a technique used to emphasize or make certain notes "jump out" of melodic phrases. There are two different types of raking techniques used in this book. The first is achieved by muting the strings near the bridge, with the palm of the right hand then striking across all the strings, to sound an already fretted note on one of the top three strings. The string that is to be sounded must not be muted. Once the targeted note is sounded, it can be bent, vibratoed, slid, etc. The second rake is performed by lightly muting the strings with the left hand fingers then raking across the strings with the right hand and sounding a note that is already fretted by the first finger. (See photo section.)

15. HYBRID PICKING

Hybrid picking is a technique where two notes on different strings are played together, either with a pick and middle finger or any two fingers. (See photo section.)

16. DOUBLE - STOPS

Double stops are two notes played together. They can be played either by using a pick or by hybrid picking.

17. BOX POSITION
A position on the guitar neck where all the notes of certain scale patterns (major pentatonic, minor pentatonic, Blues and hybrid scales) lie within a four fret span. Since all the notes in the "box position" are lined up in easy to play patterns this position lends itself to easy to visualize licks and effective improvisation usage. Its drawback is that with constant use of this position one can end up playing finger patterns without hearing the more musical and complex lines that can be created by using the whole neck and breaking away from set patterns.

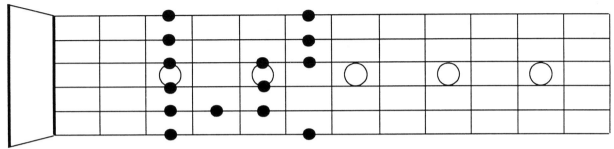

"A" BLUES SCALE

18. NINTH CHORD POSITION
A position based on a particular ninth chord shape.

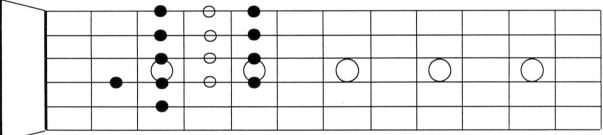

"C" NINTH CHORD PATTERN

● Chord tones.   ○ Passing tones

This position is useful for breaking out of the "box pattern," lends itself well to chromaticism and is extremely effective for building V - IV motifs.

19. B.B. KING POSITION
A position so heavily used by the great B.B. King as to become synonymous with his name. This position, including the bent notes produces the following tones : in the key of A, A (the root), B (the second), C (minor third), C# (major third), D (the fourth), E (the fifth), F# (the sixth) and G (the dominant seventh). In essence this creates a A mixolydian scale with an added minor third which produces a scale much more sophisticated than the minor pentatonic scale used by most Blues guitarists.

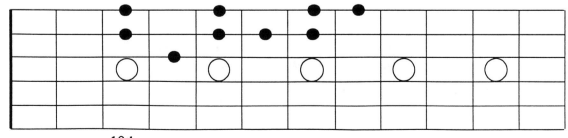

10th.
fret   **B.B. KING POSITION in the key of "A"**

9

PHOTO SECTION

These photos show the proper hand positions for string bending, vibrato, rakes and hybrid picking.

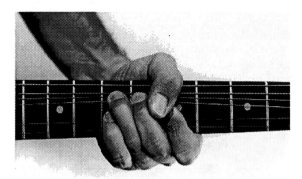

"G" string bend. Note first finger barre.

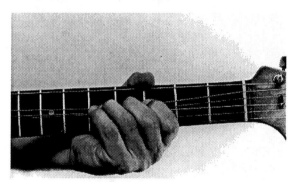

Lower string bend.

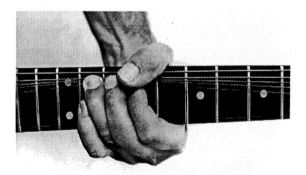

"B" string bend. Thumb touches first finger.

First finger bend

Right hand rake. Note first finger mutes "B", "D" and "G" strings.

Right hand rake palm mute.

Hybrid picking, pick and index finger.

Hybrid picking, thumb and first finger, a la Buddy Guy.

SOLO 1

Solo one demonstrates the use of motifs both rhythmically and melodically, in creating cohesive improvisations. Most importantly, the solo shows that by changing a few key notes in a melodic line, the chord changes can be effectively outlined. We will be using the same three note riff consisting of the following degrees of the dominant seventh chord, the root, third and sixth plus an occasional fifth and dominant seventh, throughout the example. On the first beat of every measure, either the third note or dominant seventh note is played. Since the third and the dominant seventh degrees are the two most important notes that define a dominant seventh chord plus its alterations, playing either one of these notes on the first beat of every measure creates a strong reinforcement of the chord structure. When this is done effectively, one should be able to hear the changes without there being any need for chordal accompaniment. This type of soloing as opposed to just playing licks or scales is a large part of the basis of this text. Extensive study and listening to great players of all genres of music will reveal this type of motific solo development and construction. This twelve bar Blues, deceptively simple in its content, begins to lay the foundation for this method of improvising.

1. The pickup into bar one is played in the A "box" position between the fifth and seventh frets. We will be using a triad shape for all I - IV chord changes. An A triad at the fifth fret, D triad at the tenth fret and an E triad at the twelfth fret. The "raking" technique that sounds the "A" note, is used throughout the solo (see photo section). This technique adds dynamics and accents to specific notes. In other words, you can make notes "jump out" of your phrases. These "rakes" were used extensively by Charlie Christian and Django Reinhardt and became a major part of B.B. King's guitar style. The "C" note at the end of the pickup is used as a passing note to the "C#", the third note of the I chord A6.

2. Measure one over the I chord A6 begins with the "C#" that ended the pickup. Next comes same lick as the pickup motif with the exception of "B".

3. Measure two, now over the IV chord D9, begins with "C" the dominant seventh degree of the D9 chord. This idea of going from the third degree "C#" of the I chord to the dominant seventh degree of the IV chord is extremely important. This half step change is the most effective way of outlining the I chord going to the IV chord. Once again, these two notes virtually define their respective chords. Since the I to IV chord change is found in every Blues progression, learning how to use this half step change is an imporant key element in improvising. You will find many examples and variations of this idea throughout this text. Measure two ends with the same pickup motif that preceded it.

4. Measure three over the I chord, builds on the motif in measure one by adding the fifth note "E" the sixth note "F#" followed by a half step bend from "F#" seventh fret B string that sounds a "G" note the dominant seventh of the A6 chord. Since both these notes are contained in the dominant seventh chord harmony, this bend, from the sixth to the dominant seventh is another valuable improvisational resource.

5. The lick in measure three, still over the I chord, resolves in measure four with "E" the fifth degree of an A dominant seventh chord. Once again we have a chord tone on the first or "the strong beat" of the measure.

6. The second half of bar four, all of bar five and the first half of bar six have the exact same motif as contained in the pickup in bar one, only now over the IV chord in the tenth position, played twice.

7. The last half of bar six, all of bar seven and the first half of bar eight have the same exact A6 chord motif as the last half of bar two, all of bar three and the first half of bar four.

8. The second half of bar eight and the first half of bar nine move to the twelfth position and the same motif is used for the V chord E9.

9. The second half of bar nine and the first half of bar ten move to the tenth position for the IV chord motif.

10. The second half of bar ten and all of bar eleven move back to the fifth position and repeat the earlier I chord motif found in the second half of measure two and all of measure three.

11. The solo ends in bar twelve over a I - V chord turnaround. The final lick consists of "D" the fourth degree, "C" the flat third degree and "C#" the major third. This lick plays around"the C#", using a note above and below it. This type of sound creates tension and resolution. The final note "E" is the root of the V chord E9.

Solo 1

composed by
Barry Levenson

13

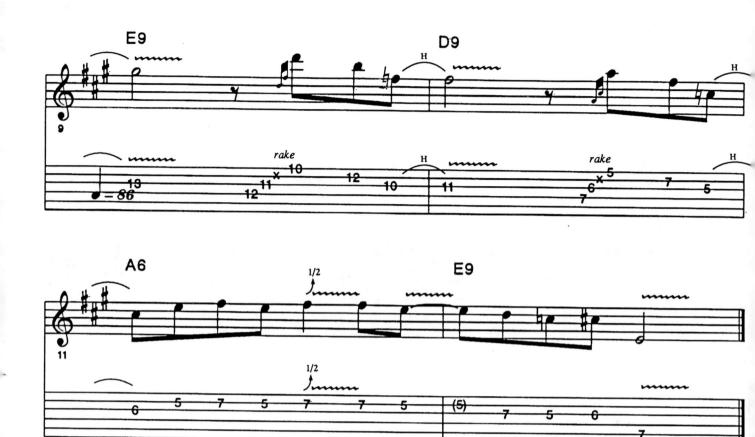

SOLO 2

In this solo example as in example one, we take a short melodic phrase and work it through a twelve bar Blues, targeting key notes, i.e., the major third of the I chord and the dominant seventh of the IV chord. As we explained in solo example one, the major third and the dominant seventh notes are the strongest tones used in defining chords. The basic phrase used in this example is derived from some of the notes of an A13 chord F# (the 13th), A (the root), B(the 9th), and C#(the major 3rd.). When these same notes (with the exception of C# which we change to C natural) are played over the IV chord D9, we have F# (the major 3rd), A (the fifth), B (the sixth), and C (dominant 7th). All these notes are compatible with the D dominant seventh chord harmony. In this example we will be bending to our target notes so take care in maintaining accuracy in bending in tune, the whole step and half step bends.

1. In bar one over the I chord A9, we have our basic lick with the whole step bend from "B" the ninth to "C#" the major third of the I chord.

2. In measure two over the IV chord D9, we have the same lick except with a half step bend from "B" to "C" giving us the dominant seventh note of the IV chord. Thus by changing one note, we create the sound of I to IV.

3. In measure three over the I chord we have the same lick again with our whole step bend with the addition of the resolution to an "A", the root of the I chord giving more reinforcement to the I chord tonality.

4. Measure four is still over the I chord and contains the note "A" carried over from the previous measure. This gives us a pause in our solo.

5. Measures five and six are over the IV chord D7 and simply repeat the motif from measure two with a half step bend that targets "C" the dominant seventh note.

6. Measures seven and eight over the I chord, repeat measures three and four.

7. Measure nine over the V chord E9, has the same interval degrees as our basic lick and utilizes the same whole step bend from the ninth to the major third in this case "F#" to "G#".

8. Measure ten, like measure nine, has the same interval degrees as our basic lick only over the IV chord D9 and utilizes the whole step bend from the ninth to the third, in this case "E" to "F#".

9. Measure eleven over the I chord uses the same basic lick played down one octave to match the register of the previous V - IV licks.

10. Measure twelve over the V chord resolves to "E" the root of the V chord E9.

This example demonstrates how a simple melodic phrase can be altered to create a melodically strong solo statement. By knowing how to target the major third and dominant seventh notes of the chords we are improvizing over, we can easily outline chord changes and control the melodic content and structure of our solos. Using this solo as a basic formula, experiment with your own melodic phrases altering the key notes accordingly to fit the I - IV - V changes. Use different octave registers, bends, rhythmic variations, vibratos, etc., for variation. Do not be afraid to use simple lines, for there is beauty to be found in simplicity.

Solo 2

composed by
Barry Levenson

16

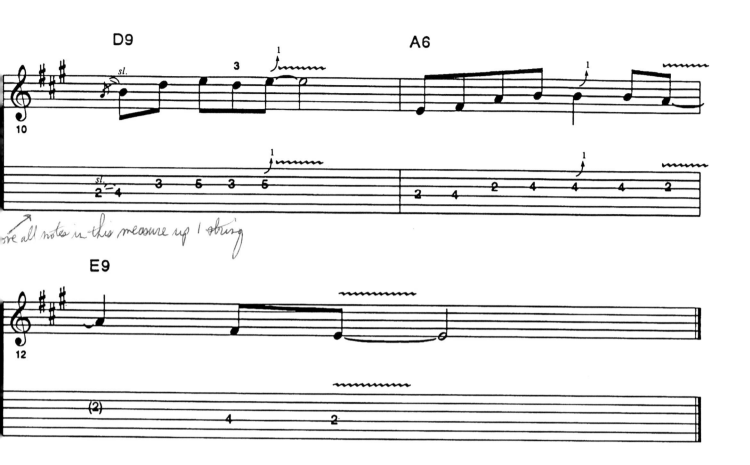

move all notes in this measure up 1 string

SOLO 3

This solo continues our study of motific development and elaborates on the use of " target notes" to reinforce chordal harmony.

1. The run in measure one over the I chord A6, is played in the A "box" position between the fifth and seventh frets. The first two triplets are comprised of notes from the A minor pentatonic scale. The second triplet ends with "D" the fourth degree followed by "C" the third degree before targeting "C#" the third degree. This idea of playing a note below and a note above the major third of a chord or, visa versa, is useful for setting up the target note, in this case the "C#".

2. Measure two over the IV chord D9, builds on the motif in measure one by using the same lick only ending on "C". Since "C" is the dominant seventh degree of D7 we have our major third of the I chord to the dominant seventh of the IV chord change that was introduced in solo number one.

3. The two bar lick over the I chord in measures three and four continues the motific development of this solo by copying the first two triplets of the previous measures before introducing a new idea into the line. The lick continues with an A minor pentatonic pattern using notes above and below the major third degree "C#" (as discussed in measure one) before targeting the "C#" on the first beat of bar four.

4. Bar four has another targeting idea- a chromatic run of "A" and "G#" leading to another important chord tone, the dominant seventh note "G". Continuing the idea of playing notes above and below the major third degree of a chord, the last eighth note of measure four is an "F" the flat third of a D9 chord and is used to approach the "F#" the major third that begins measure five.

5. Measure five over the IV chord D9, incorporates the chord tones "F#" the major third, "A" the fifth, "B" the sixth and "C" the dominant seventh. The "B" is bent up to the "C" giving us the bend from the sixth to the dominant seventh.

6. Measure six still over the IV chord, starts with "F#" the major third that was targeted by the pickup "F" in measure five. Next, we introduce a new idea in motific development: The "C" that was targeted in measure five is targeted again now in measure six, only now played one octave down. This creates a resolution to this two bar phrase. Study this idea and experiment with it. Play a lick, end it with a chord tone- follow it with the same lick but end it with the same note one octave down. This concept makes for logical sounding lines that have a sense of rightness in their resolution.

7. Measure seven back over the I chord, explores the previous idea even further. Since measure six ended on the dominant seventh note of the IV chord, the note "C", we begin measure seven by playing the dominant seventh note of the I chord the note "G". Beginning a measure on the same degree of the scale of the previous measure, only over a different chord, is very effective in building a strong melodic line. Measure seven continues with a mostly A major pentatonic line that resolves in measure eight.

8. The two bar I chord lick that began in measure seven resolves in measure eight with another improvising concept; ending a phrase with the same chord tone that began it, played one octave up or down, in this case "G" the dominant seventh degree one octave down. The chromatic run "A"and "G#" that targets the "G" also refers back to the chromatic target run in measure four only played one octave down.

9. Measure nine over the V chord E9, is played out of our "ninth" chord position at the seventh fret. Note that we ended measure eight with "G" the dominant seventh degree of the I chord and we start measure nine with the major third degree of the five chord "G#". This half step interval once again builds a strong melodic line. Next we have our "chromatic target theme" that appears throughout the solo. We target the dominant seventh degree with the notes "E" and "Eb".

10. Measure ten over the IV chord, is exactly the same as measure nine, only one step down. This creates a strong V - IV motif. The idea of playing a V chord lick followed by the identical same lick (only using the intervals of the IV chord) is another valuable improvising concept and one that will crop up frequently in this text.

11. Measures eleven and twelve over a I - V - I - IV turnaround utilizes a complex but very effective targeting concept. The I chord A9 is targeted with the major third "C#" on the second beat, the IV chord D9 is targeted with the root note "D" on the third beat and reinforced with a flatflat third to the major third "F" to"F#".

12. The turnaround continues with the I chord A9, targeted with the root "A" on the first beat and the V chord E9 is targeted with a bend from "D" to "E", the root note. All strong chord tones are targeted on strong beats giving a melodic outline that stands on its own with or without chordal accompaniment. Using chord tones that fall on the downbeat of chord changes can be useful in navigating through rapid chord progressions.

Analyzing a solo for its form and content can be a valuable asset.

AUTHORS NOTE

At this point, I would like to state that some of these concepts may seem too complex to assimilate into one's playing immediately. I frequently hear from my students the words "I can't think that fast" but be assured that with patience, practice and study, your improvisational abilities and your ear will improve and these concepts will begin to appear in your playing.

Solo 3

composed by
Barry Levenson

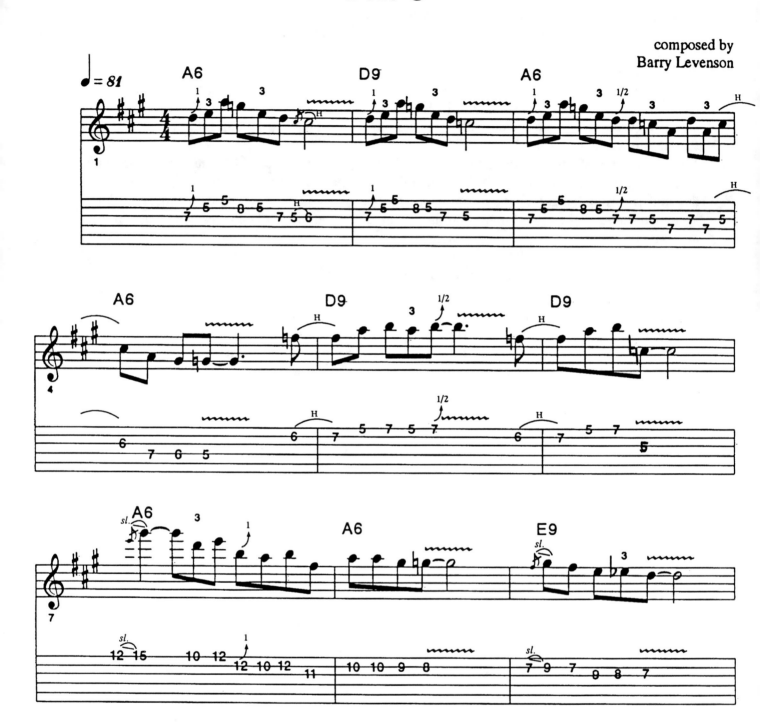

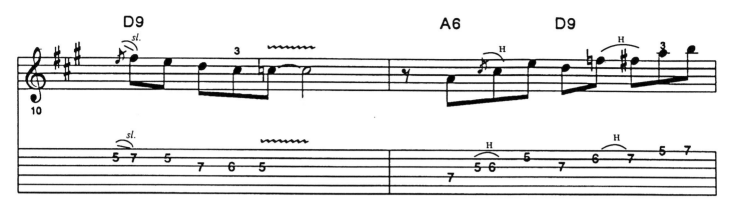

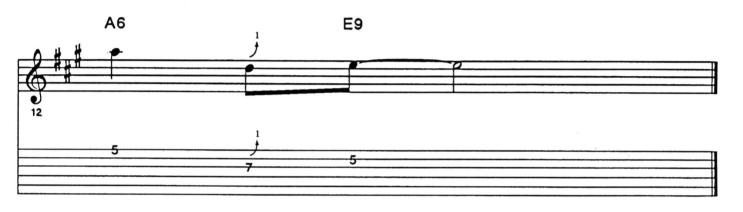

SOLO 4

This solo explores the concept of phrasing i.e. rhythmic placement of notes as applied to Blues soloing. Many players have a vocabulary of licks and scales but have little understanding or regard to rhythmic placement of the notes that they play. Improvisations must go hand in hand with the rhythmical aspect of the music that is being played over. Great melodic ideas without proper phrasing are ineffective. Phrasing can be compared to human speech. A person who rambles on continuously without stopping is sure to loose the attention of his or her listener and likewise someone who pauses interminably between words or sentences will do the same. Many students wonder why their improvisations sound disjointed, the reason being that their solos are played out of rhythm, they "fight" or go against the flow of the music. This exercise is designed to give the aspiring player a foundation upon which to build the correct fundamentals of good phrasing. Short concise statements with proper rhythmic intent along with a good understanding of melodic structuring are the cornerstones of great soloing regardless of the genre of music. In this example, we will be targeting the first or downbeat of every measure with a sustaining chord tone, usually a dotted half note followed by a triplet or a two eighth note pickup leading into the following measure. This style of phrasing when mastered, will enable one to get locked into the rhythm of the music or "get in the pocket." Once this is understood it becomes easier to elaborate on this idea and correct phrasing will become second nature. Once again I cannot stress too lightly the importance of listening to the masters of the Blues idiom. B.B. King, for instance can turn a four note lick into a complete musical statement with his impeccable sense of phrasing and timing as can Albert King, T-Bone Walker, Buddy Guy etc. Study of this solo will go a long way to opening the door to one of the key elements of good soloing, phrasing!

1. The pickup measure contains a stock G "box" lick that sets the phrasing motif for the entire solo. The "unison slide" from "G" the root third fret E string to "G" eighth fret B string lands on the downbeat of the first measure locking us in with the rhythm of the music. Thus, every downbeat will have a sustained chord tone which allows the music to "breathe" and the last beat of each measure will act as the pickup into the following measure. To reiterate, a sustained chord tone followed by a triplet or two eighth notes that become the pickup for the next measure. This can be counted in the following manner.

4 and a   1 2 3   4 and a   etc.

2. The pickup in measure one lands on "G" the root in measure two. Measure two moves to the eighth fret the "B.B. King " position for a major pentatonic lick that targets "B" the third, with a whole step bend in measure three.

3. Measure three has the sustained "B" note followed by two eighth notes that target "G" the root note in measure four. Note the use of "rakes" for accents.

4. The pickup in measure four outlines the IV chord C9 with the lick based on a C triad shape "E" the third, "G" the fifth and "C" the root that targets "Bb," the dominant seventh note in measure five.

5. Measure five's pickup, a variation on the previous pickup, targets the dominant seventh again in measure six with a half step bend from the sixth to the flatted seventh.

6. The sixth measure, back over the G9 chord has a pickup played at the fifteenth fret based on a G triad shape "B" the third, "D" the fifth and "G" the root, that targets the root with a whole step bend from "F" the dominant seventh to "G" the root in measure seven.

7. The pickup in measure seven slides back down to the G "box" at the third fret and targets the root in measure eight.

8. The pickup in measure eight utilizes "F" the flat third, "F#" the major third and "A" the fifth of the V chord D9 and targets the "C" the dominant seventh in measure nine with a half step bend from the sixth to the seventh.

9. The pickup in measure nine uses the same interval degrees as the preceeding measure only over the IV chord C9. This targets "Bb" the dominant seventh in measure ten.

10. Measure tens pickup targets "G" the root in measure eleven.

11. Measure elevens pickup is the same lick as the preceeding measure, only one octave down and targets "G" the root in measure twelve.

12. Measure twelve has the root "G" followed by a minor pentatonic plus chromatic turnaround that resolves to "D" the root of the V chord.

Solo 4

composed by
Barry Levenson

24

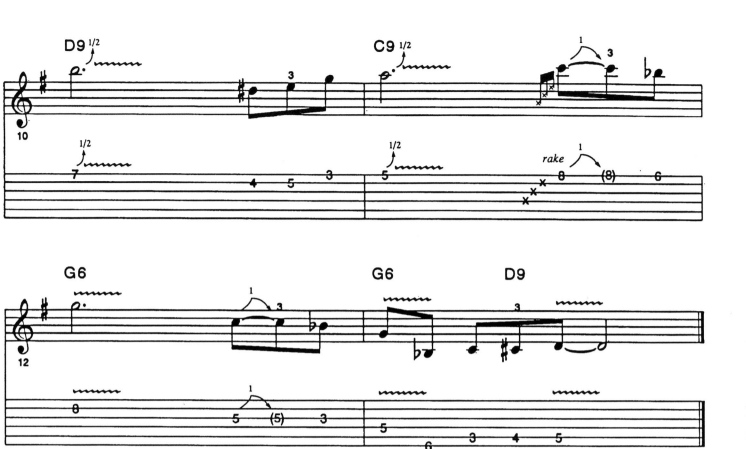

SOLO 5

Since the very beginning of Blues guitar, both acoustic and electric, double - stops, ie. two notes played simulatneously, have been used to great effect both in solo and accompaniment playing. Double - stops add fullness, punctuation, outline chordal harmony, make great comping patterns and adds dynamics to the music. This solo example is based completely on the study of double - stops as applied to a twelve bar Blues. Experiment and permutate the ideas presented in this example and add double stop ideas to your playing. A later text will cover an in depth look at the myriad uses of double stops.

1. The double - stops in measure one, based on the interval of a flat five (the notes F# and C) are played in a triplet rhythm. They resolve to the fifth "E" and the root "A" of the I chord. This flat fifth interval double - stop is heard in the playing of every Blues guitarist and is an effective tension builder.

2. This same rhythmic and melodic pattern is now played over the IV chord in measure two with the resolution now being to the dominant seventh "C" and the ninth "E" of the IV chord, thereby effectively setting up a : I - IV change.

3. This motif is again played in measure three, with twice the amount of triplets, before resolving to the I chord in bar four. The doubling up of the triplet pattern builds upon the tension created by the triplet rhythms of bars one and two.

4. The I chord resolution in bar four is treated by playing the double - stop, root "A" fifth fret E string and the fifth "E" fifth fret B string of the I chord. The double - stop fourth, "D" seventh fret G string and the sixth, "F#" seventh fret B string set up momentarily, a suspension before the flat third "C" fifth fret G string and the fifth fret B string is hammered to the third "C#" sixth fret G string. The root note "A" seventh fret G string combined with the above mentioned double - stop spells out an "A" triad. The last eighth note of the measure "D" twelfth fret D string is the root note of the IV chord. This "early signaling" of an approaching chord change was one of the musical inventions of the early Be Bop pioneers, Charlie Christian in particular.

5. The hammer - on double - stop motif in measure four is now carried over to the IV chord in measure five, only now played in the tenth position.

6. The double - stops for the IV chord are now played in a sequence consisting of the third "F#" eleventh fret G string and the fifth "A" tenth fret B string. These are now moved down a whole step to the ninth "E" ninth fret G string and the fourth "G" eighth fret B string. They now move to the fifth position with the double - stops root "D" seventh fret G string and the third "F#" seventh fret B string. This shape now moves down a half step to the sixth fret and finally resolves on the fifth fret to the seventh "C" fifth fret G string and the ninth "E" fifth fret B string. The last three double - stops are played out of the "ninth chord" position on the fourth and fifth frets. See diagram. This run was a favourite of the undisputed "double - stop king" Chuck Berry.

7. Bar seven refers back to the motif in bar three.

8. Bar eight refers back to the motif in bar four.

9. The pickup note "B" ninth fret D string, the fifth of the V chord refers back to the ideas presented in bar four. This leads us into a series of double - stops based on the V chord E7. This run starts with the notes "D" seventh fret G string and "F#" seventh fret B string, the seventh and ninth degrees of the E9 chord. They then move up a half step to the eighth fret to keep the continuity of the triplet rhythm that ends with "E" ninth fret G string and "G#" ninth fret B string, the root and third respectively of the E9 chord. The next triplet is based on the interval of a perfect fourth and is played on the seventh, eighth and ninth frets on the B and E strings finally resolving to the double - stop "F#" seventh fret B string and "B" seventh fret E string the ninth and fifth of the E9 chord. The pickup note "A" seventh fret D string the fifth note of the IV chord D9 again refers back to the ideas presented in bar four.

10. The triplet run in bar ten mirrors the motif in bar nine and has the same interval relationship only now over the IV chord D9. Measures nine and ten create a V - IV motif.

11. The I and IV chord triplets are created with our now familiar lick based on the pentatonic "box" position between the fifth and seventh frets. This is followed by a double - stop "D" seventh fret G string and "F#" seventh fret B string. The root and third respectively of the IV chord is bent up a half step with the third finger barre. This lick is a staple of Chuck Berry and is widely used by Eric Clapton.

12. The I and V chord changes in bar twelve are treated with a double - stop trill from "C" fifth fret G string, the minor third of the I chord and "E" fifth fret B string, the fifth of the I chord hammered to the "C#" sixth fret G string, the third of the I chord. This is followed by an A minor pentatonic run that resolves to "E" the root of the V chord seventh fret D string.

Solo 5

composed by
Barry Levenson

28

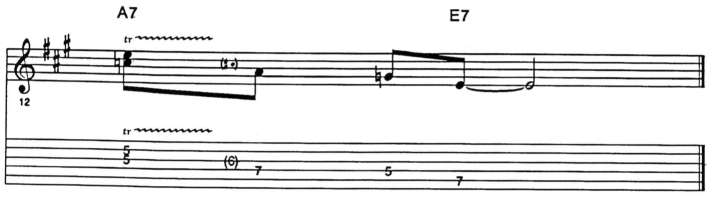

29

SOLO 6

1. The double - stop triplet lick in measure one has its origins in the "Delta Blues" style of playing. The half step bend on "G" eighth fret B string falls between the major and minor third of the I chord E7. This "in between" tonality gives a decidedly "Bluesy" sound. The low E string punctuation at the end of the measure is a throwback to the Mississippi Delta and Country Blues guitarists who accompanied themselves while singing, with open droning strings that gave the illusion of more than one guitar and bass. The undisputed master of this idiom was the great Robert Johnson.

2. The second measure, over the IV chord, A7, moves to the fifth position with a "ninth" chord run plus the passing note "Bb." Once again, this lick is a stock phrase used by such great players as Jimmie Rogers (with Muddy Waters) and Robert Jr. Lockwood (with Little Walter).

3. This double - stop lick in measure three over the I chord is a staple of every Blues guitarist and can be heard in virtually every Stevie Ray Vaughan solo. The lick uses the notes "B" fourth fret G string and "D" third fret B string, the fifth and seventh degrees respectively of an E7 chord. After the third triplet is played, the backwards slide to "A" second fret G string to the open string G moves the lick to the first or open position.

4. The previous lick concludes in measure four, with an E major, E minor pentatonic hybrid run that occurs from the trilling between the "G," minor third open G string and and "G#" major third first fret G string.

5. The lick in measure five over the IV chord moves to the "A" box position between the fifth and seventh frets. This is essentially an A blues scale phrase that ends with a whole step bend from "G" eighth fret B string seventh degree to the root note "A."

6. The previous lick is answered in measure six by playing essentially the same run as measure five. The only difference being the trill from the flat third "C" fifth fret G string to the major third "C#" seventh fret G string. These two measures together create a "call and response" type phrasing that works well as a two bar lick.

7. The double - stop lick in measure seven over the I chord is another classic Country Blues style lick. The lick is played on the high E and B strings and starts with the notes of "D" and "B" tenth and twelfth frets and moves down to "C" and "A," ninth and tenth frets.

8. The previous lick resolves in measure eight with "B" and "G" seventh and eighth frets which ends up being our opening lick from measure one. Measure eight ends with a Blues scale riff that moves down to the first position.

9. The previous lick continues targeting the V chord B7 with a trill from "A" open fifth string to "B" second fret A string. The remainder of the lick is comprised of the notes from the E Blues scale and was a stock Muddy Waters run, utilizing open strings for a "bassy rumbling effect" that was a big part of the "two guitar" sounds of the Muddy Waters Band.

10. The IV chord in bar ten continues with the E Blues scale. Note the use of the flat fifth degree and the triplet rhythm.

11. The turnaround in measure eleven starts with the resolution of the last note in measure ten "E" second fret D string and targets the I chord. The turnaround itself is a Robert Johnson lick using open strings for a ringing effect.

12. The turnaround continues in bar twelve and ends with a lick from the E Blues scale that targets the V chord B7 with the trill "A" note open A string to "B" second fret A string, the second and root degrees of the B chord.

Solo 6

composed by
Barry Levenson

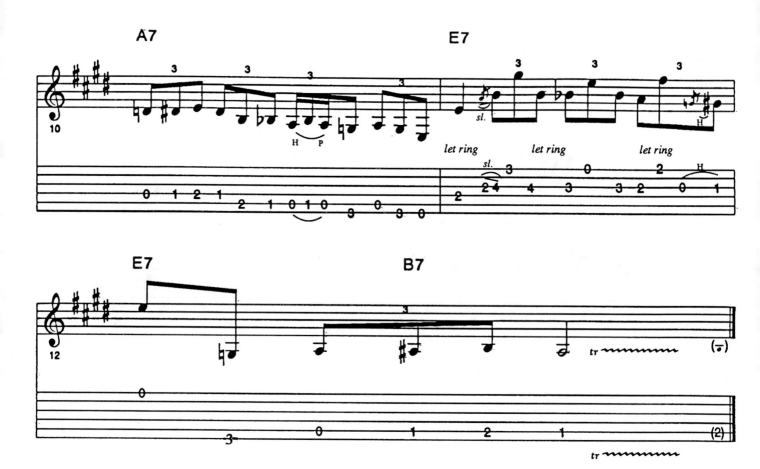

SOLO 7

This "Texas Shuffle" explores some of the techniques of the great Vaughan brothers, Stevie Ray and Jimmie and reveals their stylistic debts to T - Bone Walker and B.B. King.

1. The pickup into bar one starts with a 1/2 step bend from the fourth "D" seventh fret G string to the flat fifth "Eb." This is followed by playing the fifth "E", fifth fret, B string. Then comes our now familiar "unison slide" from the "A" note E string fifth fret to the "A" note B string tenth fret. This pickup has a twofold function : The "A" root note falls directly on the downbeat of the first measure creating 1) strong rhythmic and 2) a strong tonal intro. The quarter step bends on the "C" notes on the eighth fret E string are used to "tease the tonality" between minor and major. This "playing in the cracks" is found in the playing of virtually all Blues guitarists. The pull - off from the "A" tenth fret B string to the "G" eighth fret B string and the slide to the "E" note fifth fret B string has its origins in B.B. King but was so frequently used in the playing of S.R.V. as to almost become a trademark. This technique is a most effective way of negotiating position changes smoothly. Once again, this device coupled with the "unison slide" is found in the playing of every great Blues guitarist.

2. The I chord line in bars two and three starts with a chromatic run through the minor and major third, "C" eighth fret E string and "C#" ninth fret E string, followed by a whole step bend from the fourth "D" tenth fret E string to the fifth "E" and a repeat of our pull - off slide in measure one. This begins our motific development.

3. The second half of bar three and the first half of bar four is a hybrid major and pentatonic lick that resolves to the "E" fifth degree of the I chord.

4. The I chord line in bars five and six is a stock T - Bone Walker phrase. The "swing" triplet rhythms (see explanation), coupled with the A major and minor pentatonic scales, plus the Blues scale comprise most of the melodic content of the "Texas" style Blues players.

5. Bar six is an almost direct copy of bar five. These two measures together create a seamless flow of triplets that finally resolve in measure seven.

6. Measure seven has a trill from the flat third, "C", fifth fret G string and the five, "E", of the one chord to the third "C#" sixth fret G string. This trill outlines the I chord tonality and gives a pause from the long lines that preceeded it in measures five and six.

7. Bar eight builds upon the double-stop idea in bar seven.

8. The long triplet lines in bars nine and ten over the V and the IV chord changes refer back to the motific lines of bars five and six. This run resolves with a hammer - on from the flat third "C" eighth fret E string to the third "C#" ninth fret E string targeting the resolution back to the I chord in bar eleven.

9. The turnaround over the I chord is highlighted by two chromatic triplets, a hammer - on pull - off and a third triplet. This long line is based on the Blues scale.

Solo 7

composed by
Barry Levenson

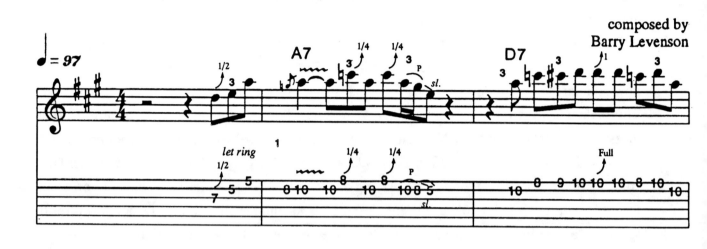

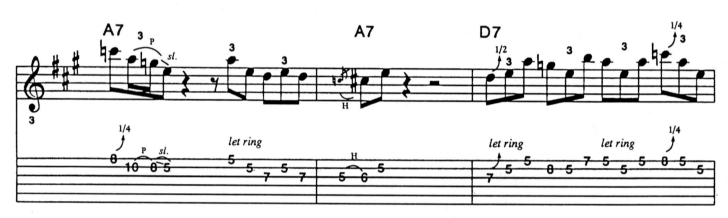

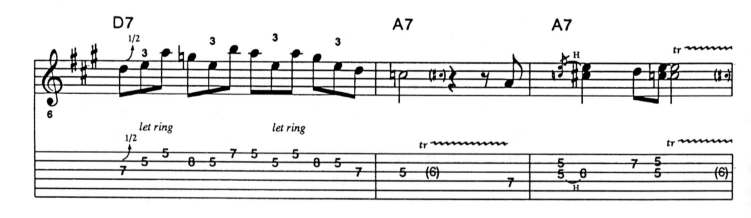

34

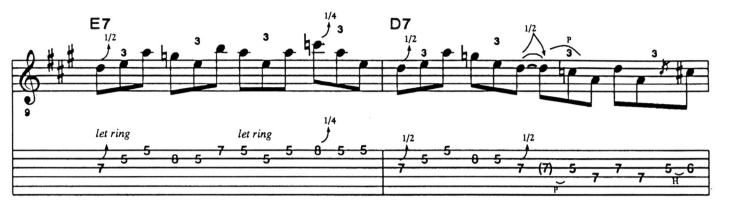

SOLO 8

As each solo example becomes more complex, we begin to mix and match some of the concepts explained in previous solo studies. In this twelve bar Blues, we explore stronger chromatic movement, different variations on the "ninth" chord position and new examples of motific development.

1. The two bar phrase contained in the pick up and the first measure is over the I chord A6. This lick utilizes the "chromatic row" idea explained earlier in the text. This row is created with notes from the A major pentatonic, A minor pentatonic and the A Blues scale. Note the wide interval jump from the "E", B string fifth fret to the "A", seventh fret D string that precedes the targeting of the third degree "C#" of the I chord.

2. The run in measure three, over the IV chord D9 is played out of the D "ninth" chord position between the fifth and seventh frets. If one can visualize this position as being superimposed over the "A box position", also between the fifth and seventh frets (see explanation), the notes that can be played over the I chord and the notes that can be played over the IV chord can be easily seen. This concept can be very useful in the treatment of I - IV changes. The run itself, although using different degrees, duplicates rhythmically the I chord run setting up an early rhythmic motif for the solo.

3. The two measure I chord run in bars three and four contain a classic Blues lick reminiscent of B.B. King's early recordings. This run contains practically every note found in the A major pentatonic, A minor pentatonic and A Blues scale. The lick starts with a whole step bend targeting the major third "C#", then moves up half a step with a bend from "C" the flat third to "D" the fourth. The "D" is then quickly released back to the flat third. This switching between the major and minor third creates a great amount of tension and sets up the rest of the run. The "release" begins with the playing of "A" the root note followed by "E" the fifth moving to the resolution to "C#"the third in measure four. This is followed by an A major pentatonic run and finally resolves on the A string with a chromatic row that ends on "C#" the major third. This complete two bar phrase should be studied thoroughly as it contains many elements of classic Blues guitar playing. The juxtaposition of major and minor third bends, a combination of hybrid scales, chromaticism and rhythmical content of the contour of the line are all highlighted in this two bar phrase.

4. Measures five and six over the IV chord D9, again use the D "ninth" chord position between the fifth and seventh frets. This lick starts with an "Ab" to "A" hammer-on, the flat fifth and fifth degrees respectively of a D dominant seventh chord. We then rake through the third and ninth degrees followed by a four note chromatic run containing the fourth, third, flat third and ninth degrees. The run continues with notes from the D9 chord, once again referring back to the flat fifth to the fifth idea that started the run. Measure six contains notes exclusively from the D9 position and resolves on "A" the fifth degree. This complete two bar run is noteworthy for its contour and rhythmical shape. The sixteenth note triplet "rake" and the long sixteenth note lines reminiscent of "Be-Bop" style phrasing. Experiment with this line. For instance, move it to the A" ninth" chord position between the twelfth and fourteenth frets for a I chord run. Permutating this lick will yield many exciting and useful melodic ideas.

5. Measures seven and eight over the I chord, refer back to the run in measures three and four. We have the same melodic content with a slight variation. Notice that so far in the solo, we "break up" our "ninth" chord position ideas with classic Blues style phrases creating a varied and interestingly developed solo.

6. Measure nine over the V chord "E9" contains another classic "ninth" chord position run. This time "E9" between the seventh and ninth frets. The use of chromaticism enables us to cram thirteen notes into one measure. Note our chromatic row ending that resolves to "G#" the major third.

7. Measure ten over the IV chord D9 moves to the D"ninth" chord position between the sixth and seventh frets. This run simply reverses the V chord line in measure nine and resolves on "A" the fifth degree. Play measures nine and ten back to back and hear how important the shape and contour of a line can be in improvising. Study and experiment with these "ninth" chord positions and create your own variations on these lines.

8. Measure eleven moves to the tenth or "B.B. King" position for a I chord A major pentatonic run Notice how the first three beats of this measure begin with a different whole step bend creating a strongly "punctuated" line.

9. Measure eleven resolves in measure twelve with a whole step bend that targets the "C#" third degree of the I chord. Our final run over the V chord E9 moves to the E "box" position between the twelfth and fourteenth frets. Starting on "F#" the sixth degree we bend up in successive half steps until we reach "E" the root note that resolves our solo.

AUTHORS NOTE.

Every measure or two measures in most of our solo examples should be studied, permutated and made part of your own playing. Take your time and study each measure thoroughly for its melodic content. The ideas and concepts in this book were written to spark your own ideas and to aid you in the art of improvization. The possibilities are endless.

Solo 8

composed by
Barry Levenson

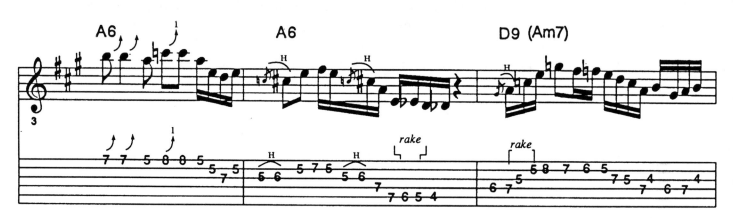

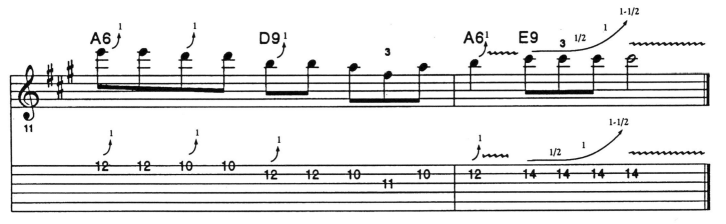

SOLO 9

1. This solo begins with a "classic" B.B. King intro, utilizing the root, third, fifth and sixth degrees of an A6 chord. This lick is essentially an A6 arpeggio beginning on the fifth degree. The whole step bend from the seventh fret E string targets the third degree "C#" on the first downbeat of the first measure. This very same lick is played again in the second half of measure one and continues over to measure two.

2. This opening lick is now played over the IV chord D9. The aforementioned whole step bend is now replaced by a half step bend that targets the note "C" the dominant seventh degree of the D9 chord. These half step target notes from the third of the I chord to the b7 of the IV chord are the most obvious method of outlining the I - IV change. This lick is followed by a hammer - on pull - off from the "A"fifth fret E string to a "B" seventh fret E string, the fifth and sixth degrees respectively of a D9 chord. Our opening motific idea is played again on the last beat of this measure.

3. The beginning of the third measure starts with a whole step bend to the major third as per our opening pickup. It continues with a series of whole step bends that are played by picking the first bend, holding the bend and sliding chromatically up the neck, creating a series of whole step bends. This run consists of the notes C#, D, Eb and E which are the 3rd., 4th., b5, and 5th degrees, respectively of the I chord. This "sliding - bending" idea is something I came across while trying to play runs on one string instead of using two or more strings. This technique gives a unique "crying " sound somewhat akin to but not quite the same as a slide guitar. There are many variations on this technique, some of which will be discussed in later volumes. The end of this measure has a flat 3rd. to major 3rd. in keeping with our A7 tonality.

4. Measure four, still over the I chord, has the same chromatic run as measure three (only backwards.) This is performed by bending the "D" note seventh fret G string one whole step, then releasing the bend a half step to an Eb, picking the Eb, releasing the bend another half step to D, picking the D and then playing the "C#" sixth fret G string with the second finger. The "C#" being the third of the A7 chord again targets the I chord tonality. This technique of bending strings a whole step or more and releasing them to the "in - between " pitches is another great characteristic, idiomatic to the electric guitar and lends itself quite well to musical and emotional expressiveness.

5. We are now back to the IV chord D7. This measure begins with a "drop bend" sequence. The ninth note "E" fifth fret B string is bent up one whole step to the third "F#" and released without picking in half step intervals ending back up on the ninth. The pickup at the end of this measure begins a slide to the third and fifth, F# and A respectively of the D9 chord. These "drop bends" can be heard to great effect in the playing of the masterful guitarists Amos Garrett and Danny Gatton.

6. The sixth measure, still over the IV chord ends with the same "drop bend" lick as in the previous measure. This measure ends with a pickup "A" seventh fret D string targeting the I chord tonality leading into measure seven.

7. The two bar lick over the I chord in measure seven gives us a look at another unique bending technique called "hybrid picking." This is played by using a pick for the notes on the G string while plucking a pedal tone, in this case "A" fifth fret E string with the right hand, middle finger. This is accomplished by laying the first finger of the left hand across the top three strings in a partial barre. The lick is essentially a chromatic run starting on "C" fifth fret G string, moving up

through the sixth and seventh frets, then bending the seventh fret half a step and not releasing the bend then bending it up another half step giving a whole step bend from the seventh fret. Each note on the G string including the half step and whole step bend from the "D" seventh fret G string is picked and at the same time the "A" note fifth fret E string is plucked. This technique was originally conceived by the great Buddy Guy and is used to great effect in the playing of Stevie Ray Vaughan and Robert Cray. "Hybrid picking" gives a piano like sound, adding a fullness to standard licks. On a historical note, Buddy Guy formulated this style of playing from listening to and playing with the late great pianist Otis Spann (see discography).

Once again, this technique has many useful variations which will be covered in a futurebook, "The Art of String Bending". This measure ends with "A" seventh fret D string, "D" seventh fret G string and then back to the "A", the root and fourth degrees of the A minor pentatonic scale.

8. Continuing on, in measure eight we have a hammer - on from the minor third "C" fifth fret G string to the major third "C#" sixth fret G string outling our I chord tonality. Next, we have "E" fifth fret B string followed by a half step bend from "F#" seventh fret B string, the sixth degree to "G" the dominant seventh note.

9. The lick in measure nine, over the V chord, is played out of the E "ninth chord" position at the seventh fret. It is played by raking the top three strings of the seventh fret, then picking "C#" the thirteenth degree of an E dominant seventh chord, followed by hammering and pulling - off from the seventh to the ninth fret E string, then we go back down through the seventh fret B and G strings followed by a chromatic run from the fifth degree "B" ninth fret D string to "G#" major third sixth fret D string. the lick ends with "E", the root, ninth fret E string to "D" the dominant seventh note, seventh fret G string. These type of licks out of the "ninth chord" shape were heard in the playing of Django Reinhardt and Charlie Christian then filtered down through T - Bone Walker to B.B. King. These type of licks have many melodic variations and uses, many of which have been covered in this book.

10. The IV chord, D9, in measure ten is treated by a slide to the major third "F#" eleventh fret G string then our now familiar half-step bend and release from the sixth to the seventh degree. This is played on the twelfth fret B string and is followed by a variation of the previous run.

11. The last run in measure ten ends with "A", the root of the I chord played on the downbeat of the tenth measure. After two beats of the I chord we have a II - V chord progression (Bm to E7). This progression is treated by playing "D" the minor third, tenth fret E string, then playing "E" twelfth fret E string pulling off to "D" and sliding to "C#" ninth fret E string. This run outline the Bm9 chord. The E7 chord is treated with the notes of the E triad.

12. The lick in measure eleven resolves in measure twelve with "A" the root of the I chord. The final chord is E13 giving a jazzy sounding resolution to this Blues.

Solo 9

composed by
Barry Levenson

* release 1/2 step and pick

* hybrid picking

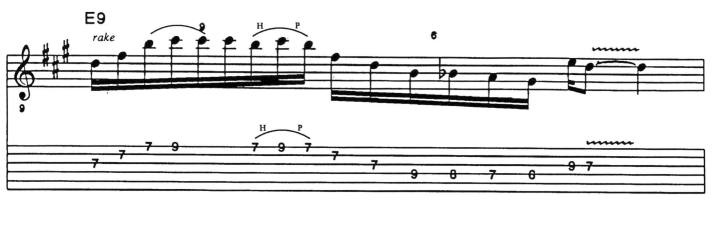

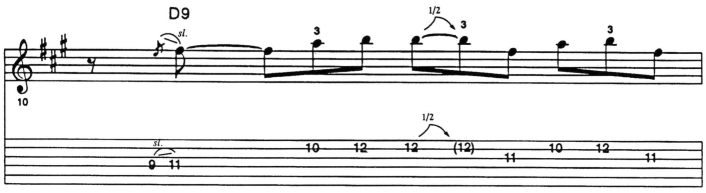

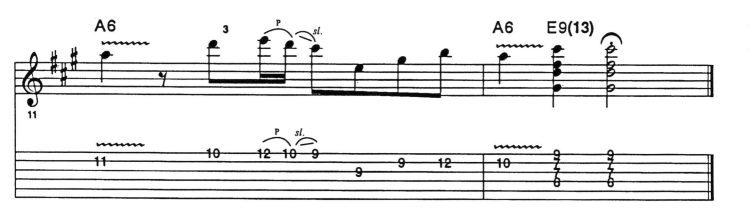

43

SOLO 10

This solo starts with a :- V - IV - I - IV - I - V turnaround before the regular I - IV - V progression begins.

1. The riff in measure one is reminiscent of the great Blues guitarist Robert Junior Lockwood who accompanied harmonica virtuoso Little Walter during the 1950's. The riff is essentially an E9 arpeggio, starting on the third of the chord. The use of the passing note "F " between the ninth "F#" and the root "E" is used to keep the rhythmic triplet motif consistent. This riff should be played in the twelfth position.

2. In measure two, the same riff is played in the tenth position over the D9 or IV chord. This is a common melodic device wherein a riff is played over the V chord and then repeated verbatim over the IV chord. Since the V and the IV chords are usually only one measure each, this type of repeated motif is a very effective way of melodically treating V to IV progressions. You will hear this technique in many great players such as: T - Bone Walker, Buddy Guy and Stevie Ray Vaughan etc. The jump from the "F#" on the eleventh fret G string to the "A" on the fifth fret E string is an example of how playing the same note on different strings is an effective way of changing positions. After the "unison slide" (see explanation of terms) from the "A" fifth fret E string to the "A" tenth fret B string (a technique used by B.B. King via Charlie Christian and Django Reinhardt). We are now ready to play the turnaround in the fifth position.

3. The turnaround in measure three is played by pedaling the "A" note fifth fret E string with the first finger, while descending chromatically on the B string from the "G" note eighth fret to the "E" note fifth fret.

4. The fourth bar has the resolution to the tonic note of the V chord "E" and the pick up note into the run in bar five. Notice the "octave jump" from the "E" fifth fret B string to the "E" seventh fret A string.

5. The I chord run in measure five is a hybrid of the pentatonic major and pentatonic minor scale, with a passing note "G#" thrown in to keep the continuity of the triplet rhythm. This triplet rhythm motif was a stock phrase in the playing of T - Bone Walker.

6. The IV chord run played in the tenth position in measure six, is essentially a D6 arpeggio followed by a bend from the sixth "B" to the dominant seventh note "C. " Since both the sixth and seventh notes are strong tones within the chord, this half step bend has a great sound when played over a dominant chord. Once again we have a pickup note into the next bar.

7. This riff is repeat of bar five and is used to begin motific development in the solo.

8. The riff in bar eight closely copies bar six including the same bend from the sixth to the seventh only now over the one chord. This riff is played in the fifth position.

9. The IV chord riff in bar nine which is played in the fifth position is executed by raking an A minor triad. This gives us the fifth, the seventh and the ninth degrees of a D9 chord. The final part of the measure is comprised of the notes of the A Blues scale. The aforementioned raking technique is heard in the playing of all Blues guitarists and once again has its origins in Charlie Christian and Django Reinhardt.

10. Bar ten has the same rake, only muted. It is followed by a "unison slide" to the fifth degree "A" tenth fret B string.

11. The I chord run in bars eleven and twelve moves to the tenth position. It starts with a 1 1/2 step "choke bend" from the fifth "E" to the seventh "G". This is then followed by a hybrid major and minor pentatonic run plus a passing note "Eb" borrowed from the Blues scale. The riff finally resolves in bar twelve with a slide to the third "C#" fourteenth fret B string and the fifth "E" twelfth fret E string of the one chord. These two notes are played in the twelfth position. The 1 1/2 step "choke bends" have their origin in B.B. King

12. The V chord riff in the fifth position is based on the root, fifth, dominant seventh and ninth degrees of an E9 chord, and is reminiscent of B.B. King's "jazzy" approach to playing over the V chord. Notice the fourth interval of the "F#" seventh fret B string to the "B" seventh fret B string.

13. The three bar run in measures thirteen to fifteen starts with a hybrid major and minor pentatonic run followed by a "unison slide" from the "A" fifth fret E string to the "A" tenth fret B string. This targets the root of the I chord. Next comes a series of three repeated triplets in the seventh position.

These triplets function as tension builders. The release comes in bar fifteen with a hammer - on from the flat third "C" eighth fret E string to the third "C#" ninth fret E string of the I chord A. This is followed by an A minor pentatonic run that ends on the root "E," ninth fret E string of the V chord.

Solo 10

composed by
Barry Levenson

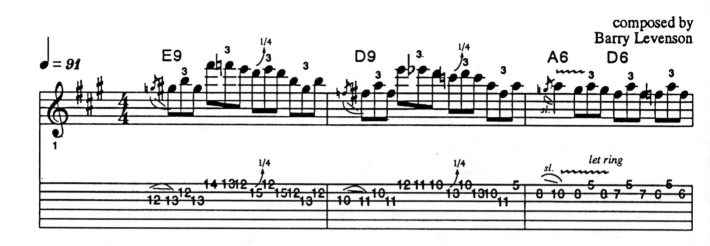

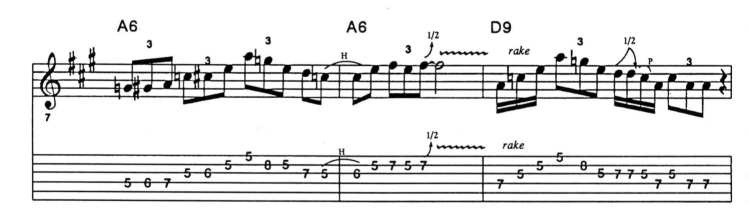

SOLO 11

This solo is based on the guitar stylings of T-Bone Walker. Called the "Grandaddy of Blues guitar," T-Bone's long jazz inflected lines, big band chord punctuations and masterful phrasing paved the way for future generations of Blues and Rock guitarists. Using almost exclusively the pentatonic "box" position, T-Bone generated an incredible amount of musical phrases and ideas. T-Bones tendency to lay back behind the beat, coupled with "rushing" the beat make his lines difficult to notate accurately. Be sure to listen closely to the recorded example. Since almost all the notes to this solo are found in the G "box" position between the third and sixth frets, I have dispensed with any note or fret positions. T-Bone's lines were based almost exclusively on three scales, the pentatonic major, pentatonic minor and Blues scale. Another component of his playing was the use of dominant chord arpeggios. Studying this solo will go a long way towards enabling one to build interesting sixteenth note lines, both rhythmically and melodically. I highly recommend listening to T-Bone Walkers body of work. To this day, T-Bones music still sounds fresh and is a testament to his genius and innovation.

1. Measure one over the I chord G9 begins with a phrase based on a G7 arpeggio from the root position (see explanation of terms).

2. In measure two over the IV chord C7, we have the same arpeggio idea as in measure 1 only now using the notes of a C7 arpeggio. These I - IV arpeggio ideas were favorites of T- Bone and since they spell out the notes of the dominant seventh chords, they are very effective material for building licks and reinforcing chordal harmony.

3. The two bar lick over the I chord in measures three and four begins with the same arpeggio motif that was stated in measures one and two and continues on with a long phrase constructed with notes from the "G"pentatonic major, minor and Blues scale. The phrase ends with a quarter tone bend from "Bb" the flat third degree. This was a favorite ending note of T-Bone's. The in between sound of not quite major or minor gave a "Bluesy" resolution to his phrases.

4. The next four measures are classic examples of T-Bones rhythmic motifs. Measure five over the IV chord C7 has one of T-Bone's favorite phrases, a G minor pentatonic lick with a slide to "Db" the flat fifth. Over a C9 chord, this "Db" gives the sound of a flat nine interval creating dissonance and tension. The "Db" on the beat, is played twice as is the "C", another one of his favorite ideas.

5. In measure four, still over the IV chord, we begin building on the motif from measure four by playing the same identical lick followed by one of T-Bone's favorite signature ideas. On the first two sixteenth notes of every beat, he plays the same note twice. Starting with "Bb" on the second beat, "C" on the third beat and "Bb" on the fourth beat this idea is continued in measure seven over the I chord, with "G" on the first beat, and "F" on the second beat. From that point, the run continues with a major - minor pentatonic plus flat fifth and resolves with a hammer - on from "Bb" the flat third to "B" the third. This targets the I chord tonality. Careful study of this four bar phrase can be valuable in creating long rhythmical lines.

6. Measure nine over the V chord contains another signature lick of his. Masterfully combining notes from the G major and minor pentatonic and mixolydian mode mixed with open strings, we have a uniquely phrased melodic triplet run that resolves to a "D" the root of the V chord.

7. The phrase in measure ten over the IV chord, refers back to the three bar phrase in measures six, seven and eight. Measure eleven over the I chord has another hybrid major - minor pentatonic plus Blues scale.

8. The last measure over a I - IV chord change continues the major - minor pentatonic idea from the previous idea. The five note chromatic run that begins the last measure with the notes "Bb", "B", "C", "C#" and "D" was another favorite idea of T-Bone's. This run can be analyzed as follows: "Bb" from the minor pentatonic, "B" from the major pentatonic, "C" from the minor pentatonic, "C#" from the Blues scale and "D" is found in all three. This "chromatic row" is another valuable tool heard in the playing of many great Blues guitarists and can be used as another source of improvising material (see explanation of terms). The final note "D" is the root of the V chord D9 and gives a strong resolution to the solo.

Solo 11

composed by
Barry Levenson

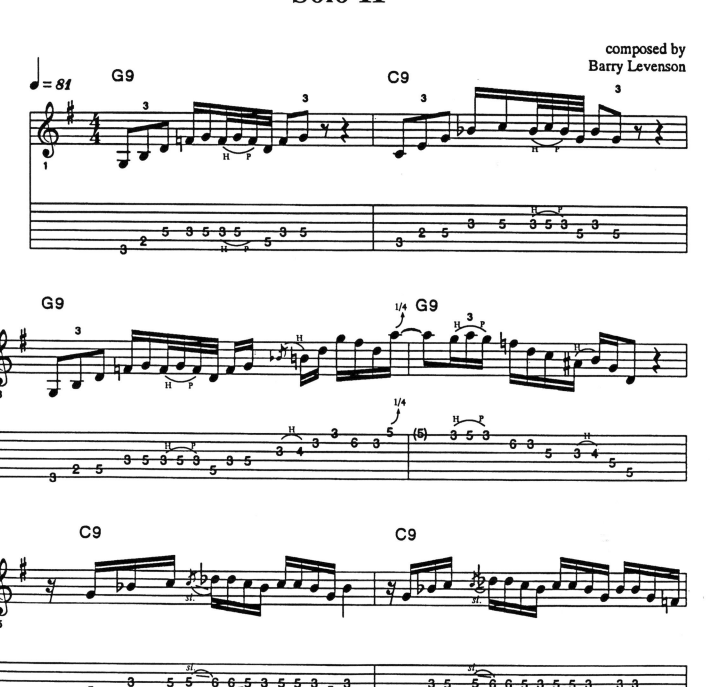

49

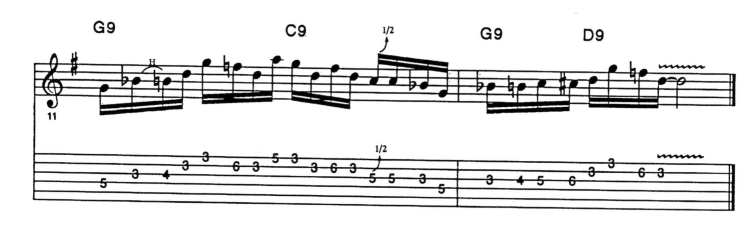

SOLO 12

This solo example is highlighted by the use of position shifting i.e. using contrasting registers of the guitar neck, a new way of building rhythmic motifs and the use of long, varied two bar phrases.

1. The pickup is played in the G "box" position at the third fret and uses a stock G pentatonic minor line before using our "sliding" technique in the first measure. This moves us to the thirteenth fret for a whole step bend from "C" the minor third to "D" the fourth.

2. The second measure over the IV chord C9 moves to the C "box" position at the eighth fret. This line is essentially a C dominant seventh arpeggio used to outline the IV chord.

3. The third measure over the I chord, jumps to the G "box" position at the fifteenth fret. We have two "rakes" on "G" the root note that are used as a punch or accent, another technique popularized by B.B. King. After the two "rakes," we jump back to the G box position for a long hybrid G pentatonic major/minor run that resolves to "B" the major third in the fourth measure.

4. The fifth and sixth measure over the IV chord introduces a new motific concept whereby a lick is played, then rhythmically copied while completely changing the notes. To explain further, measure five is comprised of a G minor pentatonic lick that resolves to "G" the fifth note of the IV chord. Measure six copies measure fives rhythm but uses the notes of the C dominant seventh chord. This concept adds to the motific development and helps create more varied solo lines. Experimenting with this idea can help one create strong two bar phrases.

5. Measure seven and eight over the I chord contains a long two bar phrase built on a G minor pentatonic motif using half step bends before targeting "B" the major third on the fourth beat of measure seven. Measure eight starts with a jump to the high E string followed by a "unison slide" which brings us to the sixth position for a G major arpeggio. This two bar phrase should be analyzed carefully for its line shape and melodic content.

6. Measure nine over the V chord D9, is played out of the D "ninth " chord position at the fifth fret.

7. Measure ten continues our V - IV motif by moving down to the C "ninth" chord position at the third fret and melodically and rhythmically copying the lick in measure nine.

8. The final two bars over the I - IV - I - V chord changes, use a I - IV motif comprised of the third, fifth and sixth degrees of their respective chords. The solo resolves in measure twelve with "D" the root note of the V chord.

Solo 12

composed by
Barry Levenson

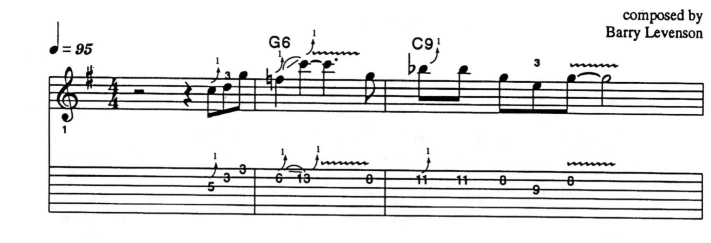

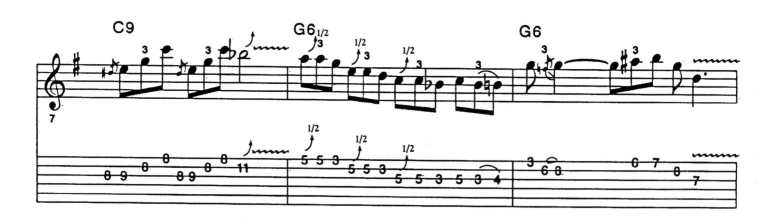

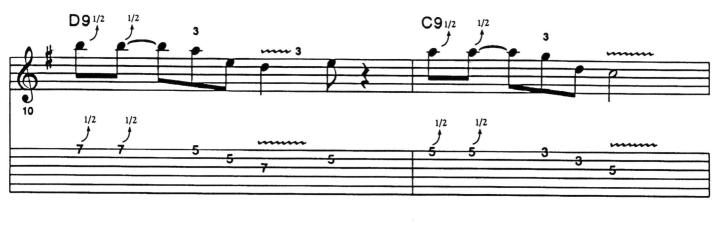

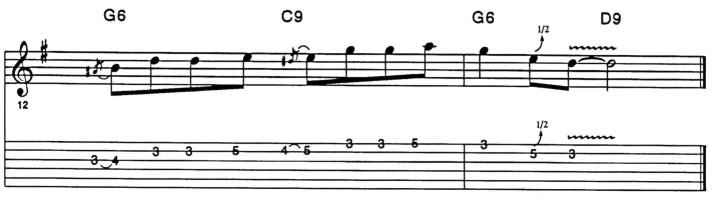

SOLO 13

1. This solo begins in the G "box" position between the third and fifth frets with a pick up that utilizes the notes from a G6 arpeggio see example. On the first beat of measure one we have a double - stop slide into "G" the third and "D" the fifth of the I chord G9. This double - stop is followed by "G". Since this is essentially a G triad, this lick clearly outlines the I chord tonality. This phrase is a favorite opening line of B.B.King and will work well over any major Blues progression. Measure one ends with the same notes as the pick up that preceeded it.

2. The end of measure one resolves in measure two, now over the IV chord C9, with a slide into the notes "Bb" the dominant seventh and "D" the ninth. This gives us our now familiar half step change from "B" the third of the I chord to "Bb" the dominant seventh of the IV chord that outlines the sound of I to IV so effectively. Measure two continues again with a three note motif that has been used as the pick up into bars one and two.

3. The motif that ends bar two continues in bar three over the I chord, with a long line built from notes from the major and minor pentatonic plus "Db" the flat fifth, borrowed from the Blues scale.

4. Bar four, still over the I chord, resolves the line in bar three with an interesting octave jump from "G" the root note fifth fret G string to a whole step bend from "F" the dominant seventh sixth fret B string. This bend gives us a "G" note one octave higher. The bend is now released without picking, with half steps and ends up back on the "F" the dominant seventh sixth fret B string. Due to the string skipping involved, these octave jumps can make for more "open sounding lines". Measure four ends with an early targeting of the IV chord C9, with a slide into "E" the third, ninth fret G string, followed by playing "C" the root note eighth fret E string. This sixth interval moves us into the C "box" position at the eighth fret.

5. Measure five over the IV chord, contiues with "Bb" the dominant seventh played on the first beat of the measure giving us a strong sense of C7. The lick continues with three notes from the major pentatonic scale, "E" the third, "A" the sixth and "G" the fifth, reinforcing the C9 tonality. The measure continues with the same lick that was started at the end of measure four and carried over to measure five. This complete phrase, from the end of measure four to the end of measure six is a classic T- Bone Walker IV chord lick.

6. As I've just stated, measure six still over the IV chord, continues over the previous run and ends with a pickup note "G" played on the fifth fret D string bringing us back to the G "box" position.

7. Measure seven over the I chord, has another hybrid major - minor plus flat five lick and resolves in measure eight as it began, with "G" the root note. This complete phrase, from the last note of measure six to measure eight, is a classic and most useful I chord run.

8. The whole note "G" in measure eight is used not only as a pause from the long lines preceeding it but sets up the long run that is played in measure nine.

9. The run in measure nine, over the V chord D9 is built from a D augmented triad; see theory section. This lick is played by fingering a D triad, holding down the chord shape, arpeggiating the three notes of the chord and then moving it up and down the neck in whole steps. Since an augmented or whole tone scale is built from whole step intervals. This lick gives the sound of three whole tone runs being played simultaneously from different degrees of the scale. This lick, again another favorite of T-Bone Walker adds tension and dissonance to the V chord. Experimenting with this idea can lead to many useful variations.

10. The IV chord lick in measure nine moves back to the C "box" position with a series of sixth intervals comprised mostly of notes from the C major pentatonic scale plus an added "Bb" the dominant seventh borrowed from the minor pentatonic. Note the rhythmical difference from measure nine. The rhythm is cut in half, giving a slowing down effect to the solo. Juxtaposing different rhythms against each other will add variety to your improvisations.

11. Measure eleven back over the I chord resolves measure ten's lick with a double stop "G" and "B", the root and third of the I chord. The "stop time" turnaround is a Robert Johnson lick played in a hybrid picking style with a "G" pedal tone on the high E string third fret and a descending chromatic line with the notes "F" third fret D string, "E" second fret D string and "Eb" first fret D string.double - stop using the notes "G" and "D" the root and fifth of the I chord. This is followed by an Eb 9 chord that resolves to our V chord D9 that ends this solo.

12. The final measure over the I - V change ends the previous measures turnaround lick with a double - stop using the notes "G" and "D" the root and fifth of the I chord. This is followed by an Eb 9 chord that resolves to our V chord D9 that ends this solo.

Solo 13

composed by
Barry Levenson

55

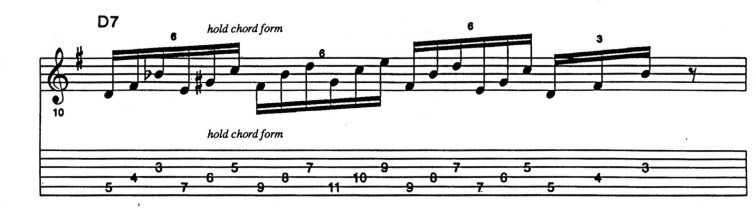

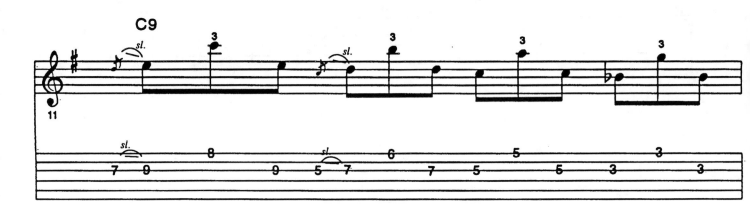

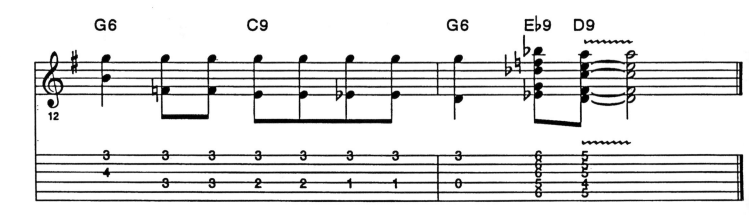

SOLO 14

In this example, we will be analyzing a "slow" Blues in the style of B.B. King, Magic Sam, Otis Rush, Buddy Guy, etc. Played properly, the "slow" Blues is a marvelous vehicle for self-expression and a favorite among musicians. Care should be taken that every note and phrase is treated with the subtle nuances of dynamics, color, i.e. vibrato, glissando, hammer-ons, pull-offs etc. Since the tempo is slow, equal care should be given to the rhythm of your phrases. This example reveals many of the techniques of the masters of this idiom.

1. The pickup measure and the first measure over the I chord C9, contains one of the most classic intro licks ever played. This lick, originally played by B.B. King, is used by virtually every Blues guitarist as a slow Blues intro. The lick comes in on the upbeat of the third beat of the first measure with the 'Eb" the minor third to "E" the major third. This is then followed by "G" the fifth, "A" the sixth and "C" the root. After "C" is played on the E string we have our "unison slide" to "C" thirteenth fret B string. This is followed by a pull-off slide that positions us back in the C "box position".

2. The second measure over the IV chord F9, moves into the major pentatonic or "B.B. King" position. As explained earlier, this position coincides with the F "box position" between the twelfth and fourteenth frets. This lick uses notes from an F9 chord and has the half step bend from "D" the sixth degree to "E" the seventh degree that was explored in our earlier examples. The lick resolves in measure three over the I chord C9, with a whole step bend from "D" to "E" the third degree of the I chord C9. Once again we are using the principle of targeting the major third of the I chord and the dominant seventh of the IV chord to reinforce the sound of the I - IV chord change.

3. The lick in measure four still over the I chord, has a major, minor, pentatonic hybrid run that emphasizes the major third three different times: first, with a slide from "D" the ninth to "E"; second, with a hammer-on from "Eb" the minor third; third, with a slide from "F" the fourth. Notice the contour of this line and how the emphasis on the major third outlines the I chord tonality.

4. Measure five over the IV chord F9, is played out of the F "ninth" chord position between the eighth and tenth frets. The lick starts with our now familiar bend from "D" the sixth to "Eb" the dominant seventh and ends on "G" the ninth degree.

5. Measure six still over the IV chord completes the motif from the previous measure by using the same lick for the first half of the measure and resolving to a chromatic idea that ends on "A" the major third.

6. Measure seven and eight over the I chord contain a classic Chicago style "Blues run" ala Buddy Guy. The rhythm of this run utilizes the "cramming" technique wherein a flurry of notes are played using different rhythmic variations. The notes in measure seven are based on the C minor pentatonic scale. Note the first finger whole step bend from the "Eb". The run continues in measure eight with a chromatic row to "E" the major third and resolves with a hammer-on to "E" one octave up. Study of this lick will give some insight to playing fast lines with very little repetition of notes. This makes for rhythmically complex and interesting sounding licks.

7. Measure nine over the V chord G9 has a whole step bend from "A" the ninth degree to "B" the major third and resolves to "F" the dominant seventh.

8. Measure ten over the IV chord continues the motif from the previous measure by moving down one whole step and bending from "G" the ninth to "A" the major third and resolving to "Eb" the dominant seventh.

9. Measures eleven and twelve are over the turnaround I-IV-I-V. This progression is treated in this manner, "E" the major third of the I chord is played over the C9, "F" the root of the IV chord is played over the F9, "G" the fifth of the I chord is played over the C9 and "G" the root is played over the G9. This "guide tone" idea is useful in outlining the faster changes that occur in this type of turnaround. Careful study should be made of the rhythms of the lines in this solo, for one of the key ingredients in a well played slow Blues is the art of phrasing. From a melodic standpoint most of the material has been based on ideas previously discussed such as "target notes", "ninth chord positions" and "chromatic rows" etc. Learning to play this solo, note for note both rhythmically and melodically will go a long way towards improving your slow Blues playing.

Solo 14

composed by
Barry Levenson

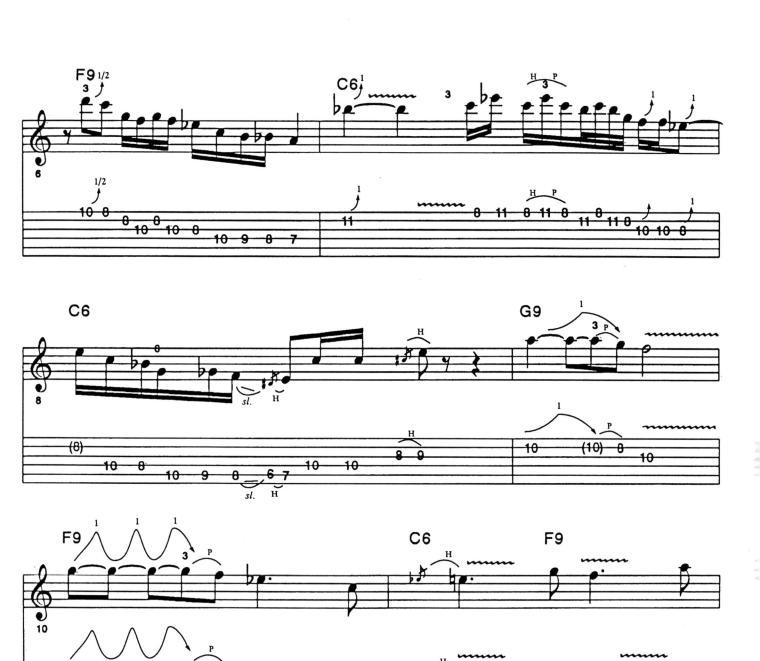

NOTATION SYMBOLS

Selected Discography

Buddy Guy
A Man And The Blues   Vanguard

Howlin' Wolf
More Real Folk Blues   Chess/MCA

Robert Johnson
The Complete Recordings   Columbia

Albert King
Live At The Filllmore   Stax

Albert King
Born Under A Bad Sign   Stax

B.B. King
Live At The Regal   MCA

Freddy King
Just Pickin'   Modern Blues

Magic Sam
West Side Soul   Delmark

Stevie Ray Vaughan & Double Trouble
In Step   Columbia

T-Bone Walker
The Complete Recordings   Mosaic

Muddy Waters
The Chess Box   Chess/MCA

Clarence Gatemouth Brown
The Original Peacock Recordings   Rounder

John Mayall's Bluesbreakers
featuring Eric Clapton   London

Otis Rush
Right Place Wrong Time   Hightone

Otis Rush
The Cobra Sessions   Jewel/Paula

Junior Wells & Buddy Guy
Live At Peppers   Vanguard

Albert Collins
Collins Mix   Point Blank

Danny Gatton
Cruisn' Deuces   Elektra

Jimi Hendrix
Blues   MCA

Robert Cray
Shame And A Sin   Mercury

Ronnie Earl
Still River   Audioquest

The Fabulous Thunderbirds
Girls Go Wild   Tacoma

Charlie Christian
The Genius Of Charlie Christian   Columbia

Doug McLeod
Ain't The Blues Evil   Fantasy

Barry Levenson/Zola Moon
Lost In The Blues   Kent